moroccan

moroccan

a culinary journey of discovery

GHILLIE BAŞAN

Love Food® is an imprint of Parragon Books Ltd

Parragon
Queen Street House
4 Queen Street
Bath BA1 1HE, UK

Copyright © Parragon Books Ltd 2007

ISBN: 978-1-4054-9563-9

Printed in China

Produced by the Bridgewater Book Company Ltd

Photography: Clive Streeter
Home economists: Angela Drake, Teresa Goldfinch, and Emma Jane Frost

Notes for the Reader

This book uses imperial, metric, and US cup measurements. Follow the same units of measurement throughout; do
not mix imperial and metric. All spoon measurements are level: teaspoons are assumed to be 5 ml, and tablespoons
are assumed to be 15 ml. Unless otherwise stated, milk is assumed to be whole, eggs and individual vegetables such as
potatoes are medium, and pepper is freshly ground black pepper. Recipes using raw or very lightly cooked eggs should
be avoided by infants, the elderly, pregnant women, convalescents, and anyone suffering from an illness. The times
given are an approximate guide only.

Contents

Introduction

Moroccan food is a feast for the senses. Famous for its fruity tagines, buttery couscous, light pastries, and fragrant and scented sweet dishes, it is a cuisine that reflects its colorful history of different people and their culinary traditions.

Located in the northwest corner of Africa, Morocco acts as a culinary gateway to the native influences of Africa, to the ancient and medieval traditions of the Arab world, and to the Andalusian flavors of southern Spain. It is a land where the medieval and the modern are atmospherically intertwined. This is true of the culinary culture too—medieval recipes with modern twists in a unique blend of the sensual and the exotic.

The Arabs, who invaded the region between the 7th and 14th centuries, brought spices, nuts, and fruits. The Moors introduced olives, tomatoes, and paprika, and Jews fleeing the Spanish Inquisition brought valuable preserving techniques. The Ottoman Turks also left their mark in the form of pie dough-making and kabobs, and later Spanish and French colonists had a lasting influence, as seen in the soups and sophisticated fish dishes, the café culture, winemaking, and language.

At the root of the Moroccan culinary tradition is the indigenous Berber population, with their simple, traditional dishes and their tagine cooking. A more elaborate style of Moroccan cooking is evident in dishes from the old imperial cities of the Berber dynasties. A legacy of the royal kitchens, these dishes echo the lavish cuisines of medieval Baghdad and Moorish Spain.

The Moroccan kitchen

The souks and the old medinas of Morocco are the lungs of the country's culinary world. Magical and enticing, filled with arresting aromas and colorful displays, they are the bustling centers of daily life. Outside Morocco, many of the ingredients required for creating authentic Moroccan recipes are available in supermarkets and specialist stores. Only a few herbs and spices indigenous to North Africa, some local tubular vegetables, and argan oil, are more difficult to come by.

Dried fruit and nuts, such as apricots, dates, prunes, figs, almonds, walnuts, and pistachios, feature frequently in tagines and couscous, fruit compotes, and sweet pastries. The principal herbs are flat-leaf parsley and cilantro, and fresh mint is used in mint tea and added to salads.

Olives and olive oil feature predominantly in the Moroccan culinary landscape. Kalamata, cracked green olives, and other varieties are offered at any time of day as a nibble or an appetizer, and they are lovingly tossed into numerous tagines. Preserved lemons are another important feature, imparting a unique, citrus burst to many dishes. The scented flavors of rose water and orange flower water are splashed liberally over fruit salads and into creamy desserts.

Tagines

Unique to North Africa and a predominant feature of Moroccan cuisine, a tagine is essentially a glorified, slow-cooked stew, deeply aromatic and full of flavor. "Tagine" is the name of both the cooked dish and the traditional earthenware cooking vessel with its majestic conical lid. Placed over a charcoal stove, a tagine enables the ingredients to cook gently in the steam that builds up inside the lid so that they remain tender and moist. Generally, a tagine will be served from the cooking vessel, or it will be transferred to a decorative serving tagine.

Couscous

Couscous is Morocco's national dish and the staple of North Africa. The word "couscous" refers to the granules as well as the recipe. The dish is extremely versatile and can be served as an accompaniment or served as a course on its own. Outside of Morocco, the most commonly available couscous is the easy-to-use, precooked variety made from semolina. It is prepared by soaking it first in water until it swells, at which point it needs to be fluffed up with a fork and aerated with your fingers and a little olive oil.

Bread

Throughout the Islamic world, bread is regarded as sacred and is never wasted. In Morocco, leftover bread is given to the poor, or to pets and livestock. In general, bread is made daily in community ovens, and in rural communities, it is served with every meal to act as a scoop and as a mop to soak up sauces. There are a variety of Moroccan breads, but the most common are flat breads, semolina buns, and baguette-style loaves.

Tea, coffee, and drinks

Morocco is well known for its mint tea, a great thirst-quencher in both hot and cold weather, and a traditional mark of hospitality. It is offered wherever you go, and it is impolite to refuse. Coffee is more of a café and restaurant drink, as it is much more expensive than tea. In the home, coffee is reserved for special occasions. The preference is for thick, black shots of coffee, prepared Turkish style, but some modern cafés serve milky coffee in the manner of café au lait.

Islam prohibits the drinking of alcohol, but since the influence of the French, Morocco has been a producer of several wines. A popular aperitif, called *mahya*, is prepared from fermented figs or dates, but the most common drinks are fruit juices and scented, floral infusions. Almond milk is a drink of hospitality, often served with dates or a sweetmeat.

Spices

Moroccan spices are varied and pungent with a heavy leaning toward ginger and cumin, both of which are held in high esteem for their digestive qualities. The two North African spice mixes, *Tabil* and *Zahtar*, also play a part in Moroccan food, but are generally sprinkled over pan-fried and grilled snacks. Perhaps the most important spice mix, though, is Morocco's *Ras el hanout*, a medley of 30 to 40 different spices combined with the floral and citrus scents of rose petals and orange peel. You can make basic versions of these spice mixes at home.

Tabil

1 oz/25 g coriander seeds

1 tbsp caraway seeds

1 tbsp garlic powder

1 tbsp chili powder or cayenne pepper

sea salt

Grind the ingredients together in a mortar with a pestle, or an electric grinder, to form a coarse powder. Store in a sealed container in a cool, dark place. Sprinkle over grilled meats and couscous.

Zahtar

1 tsp sea salt

1 tbsp dried thyme

1 tbsp ground sumac

1 tbsp toasted sesame seeds

Grind the salt from a mill into a bowl. Stir in the other ingredients and mix well. Store in a sealed container in a cool, dark place. Sprinkle over salads, grilled meats, and savory pastries.

Ras el hanout

1 tsp black peppercorns

1 tsp cloves

1 tsp nigella seeds

1 tsp allspice berries

1 small piece of mace

1 tsp ground ginger

2 tsp coriander seeds

2 tsp ground cinnamon

1 tsp dried lavender

petals of 2 scented rosebuds

Grind all the spices together in a mortar with a pestle, or an electric grinder, to form a coarse powder. Toss in the lavender and rose petals. Store in a sealed container in a cool, dark place.

Essential recipes

Preserved lemons are a trademark of Moroccan cuisine. The softened rinds and jamlike interiors impart a distinctive, citrus flavor to many tagines and salads. Lemons can be preserved in brine, oil, and vinegar, but the most traditional method employs salt and lemon juice.

Harissa is a fiery feature of the cuisines of North Africa. Generally, it is so fiery that a little goes a very long way. Wonderfully versatile, it is served as a condiment to accompany meat and fish dishes, added to marinades and sauces for a chile kick, and blended with yogurt or olive oil to make a delicious dip.

Definitely an acquired taste, *smen* is an aged butter with a rancid flavor. Set in earthenware pots and stored in a cool, dry place for months, even years, it is a feature of certain dishes and is the essential component in some tagines. You can make a mild version at home, or you can substitute it with ghee, which has a warm aroma and a nutty flavor.

Preserved lemons

5 to 6 organically grown lemons, for preserving

5 tbsp sea salt

1 to 2 lemons, for squeezing

Wash and dry the lemons for preserving. Cut a thin slice from the top and bottom of each lemon. Set each lemon on one end and make a vertical cut three-quarters of the way through the fruit, making sure that the 2 halves are still attached at the base. Fill the gap between the 2 halves with the salt and stuff the lemons into a jar, or other sealable container, so that they are squashed together.

Store the lemons in a cool place for 3 to 4 days, during which time the skins will soften.

Press the lemons down into the jar and pour in enough freshly squeezed lemon juice to cover. Store the lemons in a cool place for at least 1 month. Before using, rinse off the salt and pat dry.

Harissa

Makes roughly 9 oz/250 g

10 dried red chiles, New Mexico or horn varieties, seeded

1 tsp sea salt

4 to 5 garlic cloves, crushed

2 tsp ground cumin

1 to 2 tsp ground coriander

about $3/4$ cup olive oil, plus extra for sealing

Soak the chiles in warm water for 1 hour, or until they have softened. Drain and squeeze out the excess water.

Pound the chiles and salt in a mortar with a pestle to a paste or whiz in a blender. Beat in the garlic, cumin, coriander, and enough of the oil to form a thick paste.

Spoon the paste into a jar or other sealable container, then cover with a thin layer of oil and seal. Store the harissa in the refrigerator for up to 1 month.

Smen

Makes roughly 9 oz/250 g

1 cup unsalted butter, softened

$1/4$ cup water

$1/2$ tbsp sea salt

$1/2$ tbsp dried oregano

Beat the butter in a bowl until creamy. Put the water, salt, and oregano in a small saucepan, bring to a boil, and boil for 1 minute. Pour through a strainer on to the butter and beat well. Let the butter cool.

Knead the butter with your hands and drain off any excess water. Spoon the butter into a hot, sterilized jar and seal. Store in a cool, dry place for 4 to 6 weeks.

Appetizers
and Salads

Appetizers are often served in small portions to whet the appetite. They are beautifully presented in the form of sumptuous, creamy dips, aromatic savory pastries, spicy grilled shrimp, bite-size meatballs, and tangy, fruity salads. Nuts, olives, and delicate morsels of fruit or cheese are also served as appetizers.

Although some Moroccan salads feature raw seasonal vegetables, many are made with cooked vegetables, which are mashed to a pulp and presented as a "salad." Zesty and spicy, tart and sweet, Moroccan appetizers and salads are very tasty and refreshing.

Eggplant and tomato salad

Zahlouk

Serves 4

2 large eggplants,
peeled and cubed

2 to 3 tbsp olive or argan oil

1 to 2 tsp cumin seeds, crushed

2 to 3 garlic cloves, crushed

2 to 3 large ripe tomatoes,
peeled and chopped to a pulp

1 to 2 tsp granulated sugar

1 to 2 tsp Harissa

1 small bunch of fresh flat-leaf
parsley, finely chopped

juice of 1 lemon

salt and pepper

This dish is delicious served as a salad or as a dip with bread or crudités. The eggplants can be baked, steamed, or boiled to soften the flesh. When presenting this dish as an appetizer, serve it with chunks of crusty bread or toasted flat bread.

Put the eggplant cubes in a steamer and steam for 8 to 10 minutes, until soft. Tip onto a cutting board and mash with a fork.

Heat the oil in a heavy-bottom saucepan, add the cumin seeds and garlic, and cook over medium heat for 1 to 2 minutes, stirring, until the cumin seeds become fragrant. Add the tomatoes, sugar, Harissa, and half the parsley. Cook over low heat for 15 to 20 minutes, stirring occasionally, until the mixture resembles a thick sauce. Stir in the lemon juice and mashed eggplant until thoroughly combined and heat through. Season with salt and pepper to taste.

Let the mixture cool in the saucepan. Serve while slightly warm or at room temperature, garnished with the remaining chopped parsley.

Cook's tip
Instead of Harissa, you can use 1 teaspoon paprika mixed with 1 teaspoon ground coriander and a good pinch of cayenne pepper or chili powder.

Grapefruit and fennel salad

Salade de pamplemousse

Serves 4 to 6

2 ruby or pink grapefruit

1 tsp sea salt

1 fennel bulb

2 to 3 scallions, thinly sliced

1 tsp cumin seeds

2 to 3 tbsp olive oil

handful of black olives, for garnishing

Light and refreshing, this is a lovely hot weather salad. It is delicious served to whet the appetite or as an accompaniment to grilled meat and fish. Ruby or pink grapefruit look particularly pretty in this salad, or you could try blood oranges.

Using a knife, remove and discard the rind from the grapefruit and cut down between the membranes to remove the segments intact, discarding any seeds. Cut each segment in half, put in a bowl, and sprinkle with the salt.

Trim the fennel bulb. Cut in half lengthwise, then crosswise, and finely slice with the grain. Add to the grapefruit and toss in the scallions, cumin seeds, and oil. Garnish the salad with the olives and serve.

Garlicky fava bean dip

Bessara

Serves 4 to 6

1½ cups dried fava beans, soaked overnight in plenty of cold water

2 to 3 garlic cloves, halved

1 to 2 tsp ground cumin

1 tsp ground coriander

3 tbsp olive oil

juice of ½ lemon

salt and pepper

paprika and dried thyme or Zahtar, for garnishing

selection of crudités, for serving

This traditional fava bean dip is very popular throughout Morocco. Smooth and garlicky and sprinkled with paprika, dried thyme, or the Middle Eastern spice mix Zahtar, it is delicious served as an appetizer with toasted flat bread or crudités.

Drain the beans, remove and discard the wrinkly skins, and put in a large saucepan with just enough water to cover. Stir in the garlic, cumin, and coriander, bring the water to a boil, and boil for 5 minutes.

Reduce the heat, cover, and simmer gently for 1 hour, or until the beans are tender (top off the water if necessary during cooking).

Drain the beans and garlic, reserving the cooking liquid. While still warm, whiz the beans and garlic in a blender or food processor, adding spoonfuls of the reserved cooking liquid to prevent the mixture from becoming too stiff. Gradually blend in the oil and lemon juice to form a smooth purée. Alternatively, pound the beans and garlic in a large mortar with a pestle, adding the cooking liquid to loosen and gradually blending in the oil and lemon juice. Season with salt and pepper to taste.

Tip the purée into a serving bowl and serve while still warm or at room temperature with crudités, garnished with a sprinkling of paprika and thyme or Zahtar.

Spicy pan-fried shrimp

Langoustines piquantes

Serves 4

3 tbsp olive oil

2 to 3 garlic cloves, chopped

1 oz/25 g fresh ginger, peeled and grated

1 red or green chile, seeded and chopped

1 tsp cumin seeds

1 tsp paprika

1 lb 2 oz/500 g raw king shrimp or langoustines, peeled and tails left intact

1 bunch of fresh cilantro, finely chopped

salt and pepper

For serving

warmed flat bread

1 lemon, cut into wedges

This is a quick, easy way of preparing shrimp for a snack or appetizer. Simply serve from the cooking vessel with plenty of bread to mop up the oil and spices.

Heat the oil in a tagine or wide, heavy-bottom skillet. Stir in the garlic, ginger, chile, and cumin seeds and cook over medium heat for 1 to 2 minutes, stirring, until a lovely aroma rises from the skillet.

Add the paprika and shimp or langoustines and cook for 2 to 3 minutes, stirring, until the shrimp or langoustines have turned opaque and are just cooked. Season with salt and pepper to taste and toss in the cilantro.

Serve the shrimp or langoustines immediately with warmed flat bread and with the lemon wedges for squeezing over.

Cucumber salad with orange flower water

Khiar bil na'na

Serves 4

2 cucumbers, peeled and grated

juice of 1 orange

juice of 1/2 lemon

1 to 2 tbsp orange flower water

3 to 4 tsp sugar

1/2 tsp ground cinnamon, for sprinkling

salt

Delightful, scented, and refreshing salads like this one are often served to whet the appetite, or offered as palate cleansers between courses. This cucumber salad is also delicious served with broiled or grilled meats and fish.

Put the grated cucumbers in a nonreactive bowl. Sprinkle with salt and let weep for 10 minutes.

Using your hands, squeeze out the excess liquid, then return the cucumber to the bowl. Mix the citrus juices, orange flower water, and sugar together, then pour over the cucumber. Toss well and sprinkle with the cinnamon.

Cover and chill the salad in the refrigerator for at least 1 hour before serving.

Artichoke, orange, and radish salad

Slada l'korni

Serves 4 to 6

juice of 1 lemon

3 fresh globe artichokes

3 oranges

6 small red radishes, trimmed and finely sliced

about 12 green or kalamata olives

2 to 3 tbsp olive oil

salt and pepper

1/2 tsp paprika, for garnishing

Pleasing to the eye and refreshing before, or after, a spicy dish, this fruity salad is very popular in Morocco. If you have difficulty finding fresh globe artichokes, you can buy frozen artichoke hearts in some supermarkets.

Fill a bowl with cold water and stir in the lemon juice—this is for the trimmed artichoke bases to prevent them discoloring. To prepare the artichokes, remove the leaves and cut off the stems. Scoop out the choke and all the hairy parts, and trim the bases. Place each artichoke base in the water.

Tip the artichoke bases with the water into a deep saucepan. Bring the water to a boil, then reduce the heat and simmer gently for 10 to 15 minutes, or until tender. Drain and refresh under cold running water, then cut into thick slices.

Using a knife, remove and discard the rind from the oranges and cut down between the membranes to remove the segments of fruit intact, discarding any seeds. Put the segments in a salad bowl. Add the sliced artichokes, radishes, and olives. Pour in the oil and the remaining lemon juice and season with salt and pepper to taste. Toss the salad well and sprinkle the paprika over the top.

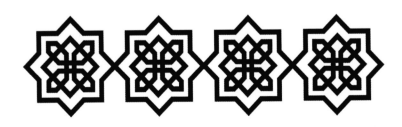

Green leaf and herb jam with olives

La confiture d'herbes

Serves 4 as a dip or spread

8 oz/225 g fresh baby
spinach leaves

handful of celery leaves

3 tbsp olive oil

2 to 3 garlic cloves, crushed

1 tsp cumin seeds

6 to 8 black olives, pitted and
finely chopped

1 large bunch of fresh flat-leaf
parsley leaves, finely chopped

1 large bunch of fresh cilantro
leaves, finely chopped

1 tsp Spanish smoked paprika

juice of 1/2 lemon

salt and pepper

crusty bread or toasted flat bread,
for serving

You can use any green leafy vegetables, such as spinach, kale, celery, and broccoli leaves, combined with fresh cilantro and flat-leaf parsley, to make this tasty Moroccan dish, which is flavored with a hint of smoked paprika.

Put the spinach and celery leaves in a steamer and steam until tender. Refresh the leaves under cold running water, drain well, and squeeze out the excess water. Put the steamed leaves on a wooden cutting board and chop to a pulp.

Heat 2 tablespoons of the oil in a tagine or heavy-bottom casserole, add the garlic and cumin seeds, and cook over medium heat for 1 to 2 minutes, stirring, until they emit a nutty aroma. Stir in the olives with the parsley and cilantro and add the paprika. Toss in the pulped spinach and celery and cook over low heat, stirring occasionally, for 10 minutes, or until the mixture is smooth and compact. Season with salt and pepper to taste and let cool.

Tip the mixture into a bowl and bind with the remaining oil and the lemon juice. Serve with fresh, crusty bread, or warm, toasted flat bread for dipping.

Cook's tip

This jam can alternatively be combined with thick, creamy plain yogurt to make a delicious dip or a herby spread for bread. It can also be used on its own as a condiment with broiled or grilled meats and fish. The jam will keep in the refrigerator in a sealed container, with a layer of olive oil on top, for up to 5 days.

Sweet potato salad with green olives

Slada batata halwa

Serves 4 to 6

3 tbsp olive or argan oil

1 red or golden onion,
coarsely chopped

1 oz/25 g fresh ginger, peeled
and grated

1 tsp cumin seeds

1 lb/450 g orange sweet potatoes,
peeled and cut into bite-size cubes

1/2 tsp paprika

8 to 10 green olives

rind of 1/2 preserved lemon, finely
chopped

juice of 1/2 lemon

1 small bunch of fresh flat-leaf
parsley, finely chopped

1 small bunch of fresh cilantro,
finely chopped

salt and pepper

In Morocco, sweet potatoes and yams are generally cooked in tagines, or enjoyed in a variety of salads. In this dish, the sweet, tender flesh is balanced with spices and the tart flavors of green olives and preserved lemon.

Heat 2 tablespoons of the oil in a tagine or heavy-bottom, flameproof casserole, add the onion, and cook over medium heat for 2 to 3 minutes, stirring frequently, until it begins to color. Add the ginger and cumin seeds and cook for 1 to 2 minutes, stirring, until fragrant.

Toss in the sweet potatoes along with the paprika and the remaining oil. Season with salt and pepper to taste and pour in enough water just to cover the bottom of the tagine or casserole. Cover and cook gently for 10 minutes, or until the sweet potato is tender but firm and the liquid has reduced.

Toss in the olives and preserved lemon rind and refresh with the lemon juice. Serve warm or at room temperature, with the parsley and cilantro scattered over.

Roasted carrot purée with feta

Slada jazar wa jban

Serves 4 to 6

1 lb 2 oz/500 g carrots, peeled and
thickly sliced

heaping 1/3 cup olive oil

2 tsp cumin seeds, toasted
and ground

4 oz/115 g feta cheese (drained
weight) or fresh firm goat cheese,
crumbled

salt and pepper

1 small bunch of fresh cilantro,
finely chopped, for garnishing

For serving

tomato salad

1 lemon, cut into wedges

This dish is best served as an appetizer with toasted flat bread. It is often
accompanied by a green salad and marinated olives. A similar dish is made with
red peppers, which are roasted and then peeled before being mashed to a purée.

Preheat the oven to 400°F/200°C. Put the carrots in an ovenproof dish, pour over the oil, and cover the dish with foil. Bake in the preheated oven for about 25 minutes.

Meanwhile, heat a dry, heavy-bottom skillet over medium-high heat. Add the cumin seeds and cook for 3 to 4 minutes, tossing the skillet frequently, until lightly toasted and fragrant. Let cool, then grind in a mortar with a pestle, or an electric grinder, to form a coarse powder.

Remove the foil from the ovenproof dish, toss in the ground cumin seeds, and bake for an additional 15 minutes, or until tender.

Mash the carrots with a fork, combining them with the oil in the dish, or whiz them to a purée in a blender or food processor. Season the purée with salt and pepper to taste and spoon into a serving dish. Scatter the crumbled feta cheese over the top and garnish with the cilantro. Serve warm or at room temperature, with a tomato salad and with lemon wedges for squeezing over.

Preserved lemon and tomato salad with capers

Salade Marocaine

Serves 4 to 6

5 to 6 large fresh tomatoes, peeled, seeded, and cut into thick strips

1 red onion, halved lengthwise, then halved crosswise and sliced with the grain

rind of 1 preserved lemon, cut into thin strips

2 to 3 tbsp olive oil

juice of 1/2 lemon

1 to 2 tbsp capers, rinsed and drained

1 small bunch of flat-leaf parsley, finely chopped

1 small bunch of fresh cilantro, finely chopped

1 small bunch of fresh mint, finely chopped

1 tsp paprika

salt and pepper

There are a variety of tomato-based salads that come under the banner "*Salade Marocaine*," particularly in the tourist areas. This particular recipe is delicious served as an appetizer to accompany other salads, dips, or savory pastries.

Put the tomatoes, onion, and preserved lemon rind in a nonreactive bowl. Add the oil and lemon juice and toss well. Season with salt and pepper to taste and set aside until ready to serve.

Just before serving, toss in the capers and herbs and scatter the paprika over the top.

Soups, Pastries, and Couscous

Bread, soups, pastries, and grilled meats are popular street fare. The hearty soup *harira* is ladled from vast cauldrons all day long, while the alluring aroma of freshly baked savory pastries, *briouat*, fills the air.

Couscous, being Morocco's staple food, is everywhere, for breakfast, lunch, or supper, and is highly versatile in both its sweet and savory forms. Begin your meal with a well-flavored soup, snack on one of the mouthwatering pastries, and serve a mound of buttery couscous with a traditional tagine or one of the grilled meat or fish dishes.

Classic lamb, chickpea, and lentil soup

Harira

Serves 4

2 to 3 tbsp olive or argan oil

2 onions, chopped

2 celery stalks, diced

2 small carrots, peeled and diced

2 to 3 garlic cloves, peeled and lightly crushed but kept whole

1 tbsp cumin seeds

1 lb/450 g lean lamb, cut into bite-size cubes

2 to 3 tsp ground turmeric

2 tsp paprika

2 tsp ground cinnamon

2 tsp granulated sugar

2 bay leaves

2 tbsp tomato paste

4 cups lamb or chicken stock

14 oz/400 g canned chopped tomatoes, drained

14 oz/400 g canned chickpeas, drained and rinsed

1/2 cup brown or green lentils, thoroughly rinsed

1 small bunch of fresh flat-leaf parsley, coarsely chopped

1 small bunch of fresh cilantro, coarsely chopped

salt and pepper

1 lemon, cut into quarters, for serving

This soup is one of the classic dishes served at religious feasts and is often prepared to break the fast during Ramadan, the month of fasting. Thick and hearty, it can be served as a meal on its own with chunky, crusty bread, flat bread, or semolina rolls.

Heat the oil in a deep, heavy-bottom saucepan, add the onions, celery, and carrots, and cook over medium heat for 2 to 3 minutes, stirring frequently, until the onions begin to color.

Add the garlic, cumin seeds, and lamb and cook, stirring, until the lamb is lightly browned all over. Add the spices, sugar, and bay leaves and stir in the tomato paste. Pour in the stock and bring to a boil. Reduce the heat, cover, and simmer for 1 hour, or until the meat is tender.

Add the tomatoes, chickpeas, and lentils and simmer gently for an additional 30 minutes, or until the lentils are soft and the soup is almost as thick as a stew. Discard the bay leaves. Season with salt and pepper to taste and toss in most of the parsley and cilantro.

Garnish with the remaining parsley and cilantro and serve the soup piping hot with lemon wedges for squeezing over.

Creamy pumpkin soup with ginger and paprika

Crème du potiron

Serves 4 to 6

1 to 2 tbsp olive oil

1 tbsp butter or ghee, plus an extra pat

1 onion, coarsely chopped

2 lb 4 oz/1 kg pumpkin, peeled, seeded, and cubed

1¹/₂ oz/40 g fresh ginger, peeled and grated

2 to 3 tsp honey

3¹/₂ cups chicken stock

2¹/₂ cups milk

1 to 2 tsp paprika

salt and pepper

During the pumpkin season in Morocco, bright pumpkins are piled up in market stalls and on donkey-drawn wooden carts, destined for a creamy soup or a spicy tagine. This lovely soup can also be made with squash.

Heat the oil with the pat of butter in a deep, heavy-bottom saucepan, add the onion, and cook over medium heat for 2 to 3 minutes, stirring frequently, until soft. Toss in the pumpkin cubes, then stir in the ginger and honey and pour in the stock. Bring to a boil, then reduce the heat, cover, and simmer for 25 minutes, or until the pumpkin is tender.

Transfer the soup to a blender or food processor and whiz to a smooth purée, or press through a strainer. Return the purée to the saucepan and stir in the milk. Bring the soup to boiling point, but do not boil, and season with salt and pepper to taste.

Melt the remaining butter in a small skillet and drizzle over the soup. Sprinkle the paprika over the top and serve piping hot.

Chicken soup with chile, mint, and couscous

Potage de poulet et couscous

Serves 4 to 6

1 to 2 tbsp olive oil

2 onions, finely chopped

1 to 2 red chiles, seeded and finely chopped

1 tsp ground cumin

1 tsp paprika

1 tsp granulated sugar

2 tsp dried mint

1 tbsp tomato paste

1/2 cup couscous

1 small bunch of fresh cilantro, finely chopped, for garnishing

1 lemon, quartered, for serving

Stock

1 organic chicken, weighing 3 lb/1.3 kg

1 onion, quartered

1 lemon, quartered

1 bunch of fresh parsley stalks

1 tsp coriander seeds

1 cinnamon stick

salt and pepper

This is another hearty soup that is best served as a meal on its own. Traditionally, the broth is made with a whole chicken, which is then torn into strips to add to the soup. Lemon wedges are often served to squeeze over the soup to refresh it.

First make the stock. Put the chicken, onion, lemon, parsley, coriander seeds, and cinnamon stick in a deep saucepan and pour in just enough water to cover. Bring to a boil, then reduce the heat, cover, and simmer for 1 hour, or until the chicken is almost falling off the bone.

Remove the chicken from the saucepan and let cool slightly. When cool enough to handle, remove the skin and tear the tender flesh into strips. Meanwhile, continue to simmer the broth until it has reduced to about 5 cups. Season with salt and pepper to taste and strain into a pitcher.

Heat the oil in the heavy-bottom saucepan, add the onions and chiles, and cook over medium heat for 2 to 3 minutes, stirring frequently, until they begin to color. Add the cumin, paprika, sugar, mint, and tomato paste and pour in the strained broth. Bring to a boil and gradually stir in the couscous. Reduce the heat and simmer for 15 minutes. Stir in the strips of chicken, check the seasoning, and simmer for an additional 5 minutes.

Garnish the soup with the cilantro and serve with the lemon quarters for squeezing over.

Fish soup with grilled peppers and harissa

Soupe de poissons

Serves 4 to 6

2 red or orange bell peppers

2 to 3 tbsp olive oil

1 onion, finely chopped

2 to 3 garlic cloves, finely chopped

1 to 2 tsp Harissa

1 small bunch of fresh flat-leaf parsley, finely chopped

3½ cups fish stock

1 glass fino sherry or white wine (optional)

14 oz/400 g canned chopped tomatoes, drained

2 lb 4 oz/1 kg firm-fleshed fish, such as cod, sea bass and/or snapper, cut into large chunks (you can add shellfish too, if you like)

salt and pepper

1 small bunch of fresh cilantro, coarsely chopped, for garnishing

In Morocco, fish rarely appears in soups. However, in some of the northern coastal areas, such as Tangier, Tetouan, and Casablanca, there are a few gems that echo the well-flavored soupy stews of the southern Mediterranean.

Using tongs, carefully hold the bell peppers directly over a gas flame, or cook under a preheated high broiler or on a barbecue, turning frequently, for 6 to 8 minutes, or until the skin buckles and burns. Put the charred peppers in a plastic bag and let sweat for 5 minutes, then hold by the stems under cold running water and peel off the skins. Put the bell peppers on a cutting board, remove the stems and seeds, and cut the flesh into thick strips. Set aside.

Heat the oil in a deep, heavy-bottom casserole or saucepan, add the onion and garlic, and cook over medium heat for 2 to 3 minutes, stirring frequently, until they begin to color. Add the Harissa and parsley and pour in the stock. Bring the liquid to a boil, then reduce the heat and simmer for 10 minutes to allow the flavors to mingle.

Add the fino sherry, if using, and the tomatoes. Gently stir in the fish chunks and the grilled peppers and bring to a boil again. Reduce the heat, season with salt and pepper to taste, and simmer for about 5 minutes to make sure that the fish is cooked through. Scatter the cilantro over the top of the soup to garnish and serve immediately.

Classic chicken pie with cinnamon

Bestilla

Serves 4 to 6

2 to 3 tbsp olive oil

7 tbsp butter

3 onions, halved lengthwise, then halved crosswise and sliced with the grain

2 garlic cloves, chopped

2 to 3 tbsp blanched almonds, chopped

1 to 2 tsp ground cinnamon, plus extra for dusting

1 tsp ground ginger

1 tsp paprika

1 tsp ground coriander

9 oz/250 g chicken fillets, cut into bite-size pieces

1 bunch of fresh flat-leaf parsley, finely chopped

1 large bunch of fresh cilantro, finely chopped

7 to 8 sheets filo dough, thawed if frozen

1 egg yolk, mixed with 1 tsp water

salt and pepper

This is a homely version of the traditional *bestilla*, an elaborate pie made with squab. Almonds or peanuts are often used in the traditional pie and the rind of bitter oranges or preserved lemons can be added to the filling.

Preheat the oven to 400°F/200°C. Heat the oil in a heavy-bottom skillet with a pat of the butter, add the onions, and cook over medium heat, stirring frequently, for 2 to 3 minutes, or until they begin to soften and color.

Stir in the garlic and almonds and cook for 2 minutes, stirring, until the almonds begin to color, then add the spices. Toss in the chicken and cook gently for 3 to 4 minutes, or until all the liquid in the saucepan has evaporated. Toss in the herbs, season with salt and pepper to taste, and let cool.

Melt the remaining butter in a small saucepan. Separate the sheets of filo dough and keep covered with a clean, damp cloth. Brush a little melted butter over the base of an ovenproof dish —a round one produces an attractive pie—and

cover with a sheet of filo dough, allowing the sides to flop over the edge. Brush the sheet of filo dough with melted butter and place another one on top. Repeat with another 2 layers.

Spread the chicken and onion mixture on top of the filo dough and fold the edges over the filling. Cover with the remaining sheets of filo dough, brushing each one with butter. Tuck the overlapping edges under the pie, as if making a bed, or arrange them attractively on top of the pie. Brush the egg yolk mixture over the top of the pie to glaze.

Bake the pie in the preheated oven for 25 minutes, or until the filo dough is puffed up and golden. Dust the top with a little extra cinnamon and serve immediately.

Classic fish pastries with chermoula

Briwat

Savory pastries filled with fish, ground meat, or goat cheese feature throughout Morocco as popular snacks or appetizers. The shapes vary, from triangles and circles to square and log-shaped parcels, but you can experiment with other shapes.

Makes 8 pastries

1 lb/450 g firm white fish fillets, such as cod or sea bass, cut into chunks

8 oz/225 g large cooked shrimp, peeled

8 sheets filo dough, thawed if frozen

4 to 5 tbsp sunflower oil

1 egg yolk, mixed with 1 tsp water

lemon wedges, for garnishing

Chermoula

5 tbsp olive oil

juice of 1 lemon

1 tsp ground cumin

1 to 2 tsp paprika

2 to 3 garlic cloves, crushed

1 red or green chile, seeded and chopped

1 large bunch of fresh flat-leaf parsley, chopped

1 large bunch of fresh cilantro, chopped

Mix all the ingredients for the chermoula together in a nonreactive bowl. Toss in the fish chunks and shrimp, cover, and let marinate in the refrigerator for 1 to 2 hours.

Preheat the oven to 350°F/180°C. Open out the sheets of filo dough, put in a pile, and keep covered with a clean, damp cloth. Lay a sheet of filo dough on the counter and brush the top with a little of the oil. Put a portion of the fish mixture in a pile in the center of the sheet. Fold over 2 sides to enclose the filling, then fold the other 2 sides over the top to form a square parcel. Brush the edges with a little water to seal. Repeat with the remaining sheets of filo dough and fish filling.

Put the pastry parcels in a lightly oiled baking dish. Brush the egg yolk mixture over the tops of the pastries to glaze. Bake in the preheated oven for 30 minutes, or until the filo dough is crisp and golden. Serve hot, straight from the oven, with lemon wedges for garnishing.

Plain, buttery couscous

Kesksou

Serves 4 to 6

1³/₄ cups couscous, rinsed and drained

¹/₂ tsp salt

1³/₄ cups warm water

2 tbsp sunflower or olive oil

2 tbsp butter, diced

Traditionally, plain, buttery couscous, piled high in a mound, is served as a dish on its own after a tagine. It is held in such high esteem that religious feasts and celebratory meals would be unthinkable without it.

Preheat the oven to 350°F/180°C. Tip the couscous into an ovenproof dish. Stir the salt into the water and then pour over the couscous. Cover and set the couscous aside to absorb the water for 10 minutes.

Drizzle the oil over the couscous. Using your fingers, rub the oil into the grains to break up the lumps and aerate them. Scatter the butter over the surface and cover with a piece of foil or wet wax paper. Bake in the preheated oven for about 15 minutes to heat through.

Fluff up the grains with a fork and serve the couscous from the dish, or tip it onto a warmed plate, piled high in a mound.

Cook's tip

For a standard measurement, 2¹/₂ cups couscous serves about 6 people. You need approximately the same volume of salted water as couscous, for example, 2¹/₂ cups couscous should be soaked in 2 to 2¹/₂ cups water.

Summer couscous with herbs and preserved lemon

Couscous d'été

Serves 4

1³/4 cups couscous

1/2 tsp salt

1³/4 cups warm water

1 to 2 tbsp olive oil

4 scallions, finely chopped
or sliced

1 bunch of fresh flat-leaf parsley,
finely chopped

1 bunch of fresh mint,
finely chopped

1 bunch of fresh cilantro
finely chopped

1 tbsp butter

1/2 preserved lemon, finely chopped

Light and summery, this couscous can be served with almost any dish. It is the perfect accompaniment to broiled or grilled fish and fish tagines, as the herbs and lemon complement fish beautifully.

Preheat the oven to 350°F/180°C. Tip the couscous into an ovenproof dish. Stir the salt into the water and then pour over the couscous. Cover and set the couscous aside to absorb the water for 10 minutes.

Drizzle the oil over the couscous. Using your fingers, rub the oil into the grains to break up the lumps and aerate them. Toss in the scallions and half the herbs. Dot the surface with the butter and cover with a piece of foil or wet wax paper. Bake in the preheated oven for about 15 minutes to heat through.

Fluff up the grains with a fork and tip the couscous into a warmed serving dish. Toss the remaining herbs into the couscous and scatter the preserved lemon over the top. Serve hot with grilled meats, fish, or vegetable dishes.

Spicy couscous with nuts, dates, and apricots

Berber kesksou

Serves 4 to 6

1³/₄ cups couscous

¹/₂ tsp salt

1³/₄ cups warm water

1 to 2 tbsp olive oil

1 to 2 tbsp ghee or butter

large pinch of saffron threads

³/₄ cup blanched almonds

³/₄ cup unsalted pistachios

1 to 2 tsp Ras el hanout

³/₄ cup moist dried dates, finely sliced

³/₄ cup plumped dried apricots, finely sliced

2 tsp ground cinnamon, for garnishing

Couscous combined with dried fruit and nuts is delicious served with grilled meats and spicy tagines. Traditionally, though, a fruity couscous would generally be dusted with cinnamon and served as a course on its own, often as a palate cleanser.

Tip the couscous into a bowl. Stir the salt into the water and then pour over the couscous. Cover and set the couscous aside to absorb the water for 10 minutes.

Drizzle the oil over the couscous. Using your fingers, rub the oil into the grains to break up the lumps and aerate them.

Heat the ghee in a heavy-bottom skillet, add the saffron, almonds, and pistachios, and cook for 1 to 2 minutes, stirring, until the nuts begin to brown and emit a nutty aroma. Stir in the Ras el hanout, toss in the dates and apricots, and cook, stirring, for 2 minutes. Toss in the couscous, mix thoroughly, and heat through.

Pile the couscous onto a warmed plate in a mound. Garnish with the cinnamon by rubbing it with your fingers to create vertical lines from the top of the mound to the base, like the spokes of a wheel. Serve immediately.

Tagines, Grills, and Roasts

Aromatic and fruity, well spiced and flavorsome, buttery and zesty—the descriptions of tagines are endlessly enticing and inspiring. From the simple peasant tagines to the elaborate versions as prepared by the imperial kitchens, tagines are easy to cook and deliciously rewarding.

Grilled and roasted meats and fish, tossed in the cilantro-based marinade chermoula, or smothered in the aged butter smen, make tasty and tender additions to any barbecue or family meal. For a truly memorable taste of Morocco, try the classic lamb tagine with apricots, prunes, and honey, or roast chicken stuffed with couscous.

Tagine of lamb with apricots, prunes, and honey

Tajine bil mashmash wal barkok

Serves 6

2 lb 4 oz/1 kg shoulder of lamb, trimmed and cubed

2 to 3 tbsp olive or argan oil

1 oz/25 g fresh ginger, peeled and chopped

large pinch of saffron threads

2 tsp ground cinnamon

1 onion, finely chopped

2 to 3 garlic cloves, chopped

1 cup plumped dried pitted prunes, soaked in lukewarm water for 1 hour

1 cup plumped dried apricots, soaked in lukewarm water for 1 hour

2 large tbsp runny honey

salt and pepper

For serving

Plain, Buttery Couscous

salad

This is arguably the best known of Morocco's traditional tagines. Succulent and hearty, warmed with spices and sweetened with honey, this dish is best served with a salad and chunks of fresh, crusty bread for mopping up the thick, syrupy sauce.

Put the lamb in a large tagine or a heavy-bottom, flameproof casserole. Add the oil, ginger, saffron, cinnamon, onion, garlic, and salt and pepper to taste. Pour in enough water to cover. Cover and simmer gently for almost 2 hours, topping off the water if necessary, until the meat is very tender.

Drain the prunes and apricots and add them to the tagine. Stir in the honey, re-cover, and simmer for an additional 30 minutes, or until the sauce has reduced. Serve hot with Plain, Buttery Couscous and a salad.

Tagine of chicken with green olives and preserved lemon

Tajine djaj bi zaytoun wal hamid

Serves 4 to 6

1 organic chicken,
weighing about 3 lb/1.3 kg

3 garlic cloves, crushed

1 small bunch of fresh cilantro,
finely chopped

juice of 1 lemon

1 tsp sea salt

3 to 4 tbsp olive oil

1 large onion, grated

1 oz/25 g fresh ginger,
peeled and grated

large pinch of saffron threads

1 tsp pepper

1 cinnamon stick

1 cup cracked green olives

rind of 2 preserved lemons,
cut into strips

2 tbsp butter

crusty bread or plain couscous,
for serving

This is a very traditional Moroccan dish, which can be made with a whole or jointed chicken. Featuring two of Morocco's most characteristic ingredients—cracked green olives and preserved lemon—it is a delightful way of cooking a chicken.

Put the chicken in a nonreactive dish. Rub the garlic, cilantro, lemon juice, and salt into the cavity of the chicken. Mix the oil, onion, ginger, saffron, and pepper together and rub the mixture over the outside of the chicken. Cover the dish and let marinate in the refrigerator for 30 minutes.

Transfer the chicken to a large tagine or heavy-bottom, flameproof casserole. Pour over the marinade juices and add enough water to come halfway up the chicken. Toss in the cinnamon stick and bring the water to a boil. Reduce the heat, cover, and simmer for 1 hour, turning the chicken over from time to time. Preheat the oven to 350°F/180°C.

Lift the chicken out of the tagine or casserole and put on a cutting board. Quickly increase the heat and boil the cooking liquid for 5 minutes, or until slightly reduced.

Return the chicken to the liquid and baste thoroughly. Scatter the olives and preserved lemon around the chicken and dot the top with butter. Cook, uncovered, in the preheated oven for 15 to 20 minutes, or until the chicken is tender and the juices run clear when a skewer is inserted into the thickest part of the meat.

Serve straight from the oven with crusty bread or plain couscous to enjoy the tangy, buttery juices.

Tagine of monkfish, potatoes, cherry tomatoes, and olives

Tajine bil samak

Serves 4 to 6

about 2 lb 4 oz/1 kg monkfish tail, cut into chunks

2 green bell peppers

about 12 small new potatoes, peeled

3 to 4 tbsp olive oil, plus extra for drizzling

4 to 5 garlic cloves, thinly sliced

about 12 cherry tomatoes

large handful of kalamata or fleshy black olives

heaping ⅓ cup water

salt and pepper

warm, crusty bread, for serving

Chermoula

2 garlic cloves

1 tsp sea salt

2 tsp ground cumin

1 tsp paprika

juice of 1 lemon

1 small bunch of fresh cilantro, coarsely chopped

1 tbsp olive oil

With its firm, meaty flesh, monkfish is ideal for tagines. Marinated in the distinctive Moroccan *chermoula*, this dish is incredibly satisfying and delicious. It is best served with bread to mop up the juices and can be accompanied by a salad.

First make the Chermoula. Pound the garlic and salt in a mortar with a pestle to a smooth paste. Add the cumin, paprika, lemon juice, and cilantro and blend with the oil. Put the monkfish in a nonreactive dish or bowl. Set aside about 1 tablespoon of the chermoula, then rub the remaining chermoula over the monkfish chunks. Cover the dish and let marinate in the refrigerator for 1 hour.

Meanwhile, using tongs, carefully hold the bell peppers directly over a gas flame, or cook under a preheated high broiler or on a barbecue, turning frequently, for about 10 minutes, or until the skin buckles and burns. Put the charred peppers in a plastic bag and let sweat for 5 minutes, then hold them by the stems under cold running water and peel off the skins. Put the bell peppers on a cutting board, remove the stems and seeds, and cut the flesh into thick strips. Set aside.

At the same time, parboil the potatoes in plenty of water for 8 minutes, or until slightly softened. Drain, refresh, and halve lengthwise.

Heat 2 to 3 tablespoons of the oil in a tagine or heavy-bottom, flameproof casserole, add the garlic, and cook over medium heat, stirring, for 1 to 2 minutes, or until it begins to color. Toss in the potatoes, tomatoes, and grilled bell peppers. Stir in the reserved tablespoon of chermoula and season with salt and pepper to taste. Put the marinated fish chunks on top of the mixture, scatter the olives around the fish, and drizzle 1 tablespoon of the oil over the top. Pour in the water, cover, and cook over medium heat for 15 minutes, or until the fish is cooked through.

Gently toss the fish with the rest of the ingredients and serve immediately, with warm, crusty bread to mop up the delectable juices.

Vegetable tagine

Tajine l'hodra

Serves 4

2 to 3 tbsp olive or argan oil

2 onions, halved and sliced with the grain

4 garlic cloves, chopped

1 oz/25 g fresh ginger, peeled and chopped

1 to 2 red chiles, seeded and chopped

1 tsp cumin seeds

1 tsp paprika

2 good-size potatoes, peeled and thickly sliced

2 good-size carrots, peeled and thickly sliced

2¹/₂ cups vegetable or chicken stock

2¹/₂ cups fresh shelled or frozen peas

1 bunch of fresh cilantro, coarsely chopped

3 to 4 tomatoes, sliced

1 tbsp butter

salt and pepper

Summer Cousous with Herbs and Preserved Lemon, or bread, for serving

A vegetable tagine is often served as a side dish to accompany the main, meat course, but among the Berber communities where meat is scarce, it may constitute the main meal with flat bread to dip into it.

Heat the oil in a tagine or heavy-bottom, flameproof casserole, add the onions, and cook over medium heat, stirring frequently, for 2 to 3 minutes until they begin to color. Add the garlic, ginger, and chiles and cook, stirring, for 1 to 2 minutes. Stir in the cumin seeds and paprika, then toss in the potatoes and carrots. Pour in the stock and bring to a boil. Reduce the heat, cover, and simmer for 10 minutes, or until the potatoes and carrots are tender but still firm. Season with salt and pepper to taste.

Preheat the oven to 400°F/200°C if using a tagine, or 350°F/180°C if using a casserole (optional—see next step).

Toss in the peas and half the cilantro. Arrange the tomato slices over the top and dot with the butter. Re-cover and cook for an additional 5 to 10 minutes. Alternatively, transfer the tagine or casserole, uncovered, to the oven and bake for 10 minutes if using a tagine or 15 minutes if using a casserole, until the tomatoes are browned on top.

Garnish with the remaining cilantro and serve hot from the tagine or casserole, with Summer Couscous with Herbs and Preserved Lemon or bread.

Kefta tagine with eggs and roasted cumin

Tajine kefta

Serves 4 to 6

1 tbsp butter

1/2 tsp salt

1/2 tsp cayenne pepper or chopped dried chiles

4 to 6 large free-range eggs

1 to 2 tsp cumin seeds, toasted and ground

1 small bunch of fresh flat-leaf parsley, coarsely chopped, for garnishing

Kefta

heaping 1 cup lean fresh ground lamb

1 onion, finely chopped

1 to 2 tsp dried mint

1 to 2 tsp Ras-el-hanout

1 small bunch of fresh flat-leaf parsley, finely chopped

salt and pepper

For serving

warm flat bread

plain yogurt

When you are walking around the food markets of Marrakesh or Fez, the enticing aroma of cooking spices will lure you to a makeshift stall where dishes like this one are being prepared. It is a popular snack or a quick, easy, everyday family meal.

First make the kefta. Put all the ingredients in a bowl and mix together thoroughly. Using your hands, knead the mixture well and slap down into the bowl to knock out the air. Mold into small, compact, bite-size balls.

Fill a tagine or shallow saucepan with water and bring to a boil. Drop in the kefta, a few at a time, and poach for 10 minutes, turning frequently so that they are cooked on all sides. Remove with a slotted spoon and drain on paper towels. Set aside about 1 1/4 cups of the cooking liquid. If not using the kefta immediately, let cool, cover, and store in the refrigerator for up to 2 to 3 days.

Pour the reserved cooking liquid into a tagine or heavy-bottom skillet and bring to a boil. Add the butter, stir in the salt and cayenne pepper, and drop in the kefta. Keep the liquid boiling until it has almost all evaporated and there is just a thin layer covering the bottom of the tagine. Crack the eggs around the kefta, cover, and let the eggs cook until the whites are just set but the yolk is still runny.

Sprinkle the toasted cumin over the top and garnish with the parsley. Serve immediately, with warm flat bread and a dollop of yogurt to cut the spice.

Cook's tip
Recipes using raw or very lightly cooked eggs should be avoided by infants, the elderly, pregnant women, convalescents, and anyone suffering from an illness.

Chicken k'dra with chickpeas

K'dra djaj

Serves 4 to 6

1 organic chicken, weighing about
3 lb/1.3 kg, cut into 6 pieces

1½ cups chickpeas, soaked
in cold water for at least 6 hours
and drained

6 onions, finely chopped

1 cinnamon stick

large pinch of saffron threads

1 tsp sea salt

1 tsp pepper

5½ tbsp butter, plus an extra pat for
browning the almonds

1 bunch of fresh flat-leaf parsley,
finely chopped

For serving

1 tbsp olive oil

¾ cup blanched almonds

1 lemon, cut into wedges

A Moroccan *k'dra* is a tagine cooked in the traditional fermented butter, *smen*. The other feature of a k'dra is the large quantity of onions. A k'dra is best served on its own, perhaps with a little bread and lemon wedges to squeeze over it.

Put the chicken in a large tagine or deep, heavy-bottom saucepan. Add the chickpeas, 2 tablespoons of the chopped onion, the cinnamon stick, saffron threads, salt, and pepper. Pour in enough water to cover the chicken and chickpeas by 1 inch/2.5 cm and bring to a boil. Reduce the heat, cover, and simmer gently for 1 hour.

Add the remaining onions with the 5½ tablespoons of butter and half the parsley, re-cover, and simmer gently for 40 minutes, or until the onions have almost formed a purée and there is very little liquid left.

Heat the oil and pat of butter in a skillet over medium-high heat, add the almonds, and cook, stirring, for 3 to 4 minutes, or until browned. Drain on paper towels.

Arrange the chicken pieces on a warmed serving dish, spoon the chickpeas and onions around them, and scatter the almonds over the top. Garnish with the remaining parsley, and serve with the lemon wedges for squeezing over the dish.

Chargrilled kabob swords

Kefta kabob

Serves 4 to 6

scant 2¼ cups fresh fine ground beef

1 onion, grated

1 to 2 tsp cumin seeds, toasted and ground

1 to 2 tsp coriander seeds, toasted and ground

1 to 2 tsp caraway seeds, crushed

1 tsp smoked paprika

½ tsp cayenne pepper or chili powder

1 tsp salt

1 small bunch of fresh flat-leaf parsley, finely chopped

1 small bunch of fresh cilantro, finely chopped

For serving

Harissa

toasted flat bread

fruity Moroccan salad

For these kabobs, you need metal skewers with wide blades, around which the meat mixture is wrapped. They are wonderful for barbecues and can be served with a dab of fiery Harissa, or with a bowl of thick, creamy plain yogurt blended with Harissa.

Mix the ground beef with all the other ingredients in a bowl. Knead well, lifting the mixture up and slapping it back into the bowl to knock out the air, until smooth and slightly sticky.

Prepare a charcoal barbecue or preheat a gas barbecue or broiler to high. Divide the mixture into 4 to 6 equal portions and mold around 4 to 6 metal kabob swords, so that they resemble sheaths. Place the kabobs on the barbecue or under the broiler and cook for 4 to 5 minutes on each side.

Serve immediately with Harissa, some flat bread, and one of the fruity salads.

Lamb kabobs with roasted tomato and cinnamon jam

Shish kabob

Traditional lamb kabobs are a classic feature of the culinary landscape throughout the Middle East and North Africa. Cooked over grills, they are delicious served with herb jam or, as in this recipe, with an aromatic tomato jam, known as *matesha masla*.

Serves 4 to 6

2 large onions

1 to 2 tsp salt

2 tsp Ras el hanout

1 tbsp olive oil

1 lb 2 oz/500 g lamb shoulder, cut into lean, bite-size chunks

stalks from 1 bunch of fresh flat-leaf parsley, for serving

Tomato and cinnamon jam

9 oz/250 g cherry tomatoes

2 to 3 tbsp olive oil

1 to 2 tsp ground cinnamon

large pinch of saffron threads

2 tsp granulated sugar

1/2 tsp sea salt

3 tbsp orange flower water

1 tbsp butter

1 small bunch of fresh flat-leaf parsley, finely chopped, for garnishing

Grate the onions into a nonreactive bowl, sprinkle with the salt, and let weep for 15 minutes.

Using your hands, tightly squeeze the onions to extract the juice. Discard the onion flesh. Stir the Ras el hanout into the onion juice and add the oil.

Toss the chunks of lamb in the onion juice marinade, cover the bowl, and let marinate in the refrigerator for 1 to 2 hours.

Meanwhile, make the tomato jam. Preheat the oven to 400°F/200°C. Put the tomatoes in an ovenproof dish and spoon over the oil. Bake in the preheated oven for 25 minutes, or until the skins begin to crinkle. Let cool slightly.

When the tomatoes are cool enough to handle, peel off the skins, return the peeled tomatoes to the oil in the dish, and sprinkle with the cinnamon, saffron, sugar, salt, and 2 tablespoons of the orange flower water.

Dot the butter around the tomatoes and return them to the oven for 10 to 15 minutes, or until they are soft enough to mash.

Use a fork to mash the tomatoes while they are still warm and beat in the remaining orange flower water. Let cool, then tip the jam into a serving bowl and garnish with the chopped parsley.

Prepare a charcoal grill or preheat a gas barbecue or broiler to high. Thread the marinated lamb chunks onto 4 to 6 metal skewers and cook for 3 to 4 minutes on each side.

Arrange the parsley on a flat serving dish and top with the freshly grilled kabobs. Serve immediately with the tomato jam.

Roasted smen-coated lamb with figs, pears, and honey

Mechoui

Serves 6

1 leg of lamb, weighing about
4 lb 8 oz/2 kg

1¼ cups water

1 glass red wine, plus a little extra
for the sauce

6 fresh figs, halved or quartered,
with the base kept intact

3 pears, quartered lengthwise and
seeds removed

1 tbsp butter

2 to 3 tbsp runny honey

salt and pepper

Plain, Buttery Couscous with
pistachios, for serving

Marinade

4 garlic cloves, chopped

1½ oz/40 g fresh ginger, chopped

1 red chile, seeded and chopped

1 tsp sea salt

1 small bunch of fresh cilantro,
chopped, plus extra for garnishing

1 small bunch of fresh flat-leaf
parsley, chopped, plus extra
for garnishing

1 to 2 tsp ground coriander

1 to 2 tsp ground cumin

3 tbsp Smen, softened butter,
or olive oil

This is a wonderful way of roasting a shoulder or leg of lamb. Traditionally a festive dish, prepared with lamb or kid, the meat is slowly roasted over the embers in a pit, or baked in an oven so that it is deliciously tender and succulent.

First make the marinade. Pound the garlic, ginger, and chile with the salt in a mortar with a pestle to form a coarse paste. Add the fresh cilantro and parsley and pound to a paste, then stir in the ground coriander and cumin. In a bowl, beat the paste into the Smen until thoroughly mixed.

Put the leg of lamb into a dish. Using a sharp knife, cut small incisions in the leg of lamb and rub the marinade all over the meat, working it into the incisions. Cover the dish and let marinate in the refrigerator for at least 2 hours.

Preheat the oven to 400°F/200°C. Transfer the leg of lamb to a roasting pan and roast in the preheated oven for 1½ hours, or until it is well browned. Remove the pan from the oven and pour the water and wine over and around the lamb. Add the figs and pears to the dish, dot with the butter, and drizzle the honey over the lamb and fruit. Return to the oven for 15 minutes, then baste the lamb and fruit and cook for an additional 10 to 15 minutes, or until the meat is cooked and the fruit is tender and slightly browned.

Let the meat rest for 20 minutes before serving. Arrange the leg of lamb with the fruit on a warmed serving platter. Bubble up the juices in the pan with an extra splash or two of wine, season with salt and pepper to taste, and pour over the meat. Garnish with chopped parsley and cilantro and serve with a mound of Plain, Buttery Couscous tossed with pistachios.

Moroccan roast chicken stuffed with couscous

Djaj m'ammar bil kesksou

Serves 4 to 6

2 garlic cloves, crushed

2 tsp dried oregano or thyme

1 to 2 tsp paprika

2 tbsp butter, softened

1 organic chicken, weighing about 3 lb 5 oz/1.5 kg

sliced-off end of 1 orange

2/3 cup chicken stock

green salad, for serving

Stuffing

heaping 1 cup couscous

about 1 cup warm water, with 1/2 tsp salt dissolved

1 tbsp olive oil

1 tsp ground cinnamon

1 tsp ground coriander

1/2 tsp ground cumin

1 tbsp runny honey

2 tbsp raisins

scant 3/4 cup dried apricots, thickly sliced

2 to 3 tbsp blanched almonds, roasted

Throughout Morocco, whole chickens are often spit-roasted, grilled, or cooked in tagines. Oven roasting tends to be the method employed in big towns and cities. Stuffed with couscous, this dish is really a meal on its own.

Preheat the oven to 350°F/180°C. First make the stuffing. Tip the couscous into a bowl and gradually pour in the water, stirring continuously so that it is evenly absorbed. Cover and set the couscous aside to absorb the water for 10 minutes.

Drizzle the oil over the couscous. Using your fingers, rub the oil into the grains to break up the lumps and aerate them. Toss in the remaining stuffing ingredients.

In a small bowl, beat the garlic, oregano, and paprika into the butter, then smear all over the chicken, inside and out. Put the chicken in a tagine or ovenproof dish and fill the cavity with as much of the couscous as you can (any leftover couscous can be heated through in the oven before serving and fluffed up with a little extra oil or butter). Seal the cavity with the slice of orange, pour the stock into the tagine or dish, and roast in the oven, basting from time to time, for 1 to 1 1/2 hours, depending on the exact size of the chicken, or until tender and the juices run clear when a skewer is inserted into the thickest part of the meat.

Let the chicken rest for 10 minutes before carving or cutting into pieces. Strain the cooking juices into a pitcher to pour over the chicken. Serve the chicken with the stuffing and any leftover couscous, and a green salad.

Sweet Pastries, Desserts, and Drinks

The traditional ending to a Moroccan meal is fresh fruit, sometimes elaborately displayed, sprinkled with nuts or herbs, and splashed with rose water or orange flower water. A wide selection of sweet, juicy fruit, including figs, watermelon, and peaches, is available and many of them are used for making fruit juices and syrups.

Sweet pastries and cakes are generally served in the home as a welcome offering with a glass of mint tea, while the Arab-inspired milk desserts and the French-influenced ice creams are enjoyed as sweet snacks or as desserts on special occasions. In true Moroccan fashion, end your meal with a glass of refreshing mint tea.

Classic "snake" pastry with almond filling

M'hanncha

Serves 6 to 8

3 to 4 sheets filo dough, thawed if frozen

2 to 3 tbsp melted butter or sunflower oil, plus extra for greasing

1 egg yolk, mixed with 1 tbsp water

Filling

9 tbsp butter, softened

¾ cup whole blanched almonds

scant 4 cups ground almonds

heaping ½ cup confectioners' sugar, plus extra for sprinkling

heaping ½ cup superfine sugar

2 tsp ground cinnamon, plus extra for decorating

1 tbsp orange flower water

Called "snake" in Arabic, this coiled pastry is the most famous in Morocco. Crisp and buttery, filled with a scented almond paste, it should be tasted at least once. Traditionally, *m'hanncha* is served as a festive dessert or sweet snack.

Preheat the oven to 350°F/180°C. First make the filling. Melt about 1 tablespoon of the butter in a small, heavy-bottom skillet, add the whole almonds, and cook over medium heat, stirring, for 2 minutes, or until browned. Drain on paper towels.

Transfer to a mortar and pound with a pestle until they resemble coarse breadcrumbs. Tip into a bowl and add the ground almonds, confectioners' sugar, superfine sugar, cinnamon, orange flower water, and the remaining butter. Using your hands, work the mixture into a smooth paste. Cover with plastic wrap and chill in the refrigerator for 30 minutes.

Open out the sheets of filo dough, put in a pile, and keep covered with a clean, damp cloth. Lay a sheet of filo dough on the counter and brush the top with a little of the melted butter. Take lumps of the almond paste and roll into fingers. Place end to end in a line, just inside the edge of the sheet of filo dough. Roll the sheet up from the top edge, tucking in the ends to prevent the filling from oozing out, to form a long tube roughly the thickness of your thumb. Repeat with the remaining sheets of filo dough until all the filling is used up.

Grease a round baking sheet or the widest sheet available. Lift up one of the filo dough tubes and gently push at both ends, like playing an accordion, to relax the dough, then coil it in the center of the sheet. Repeat with the remaining filo dough tubes, placing them end to end, forming a tight coil like a snake.

Brush the top of the pastry snake with the egg yolk mixture and bake in the preheated oven for 30 to 35 minutes, until crisp and browned.

Remove from the oven and sprinkle liberally with confectioners' sugar. Decorate the top by rubbing cinnamon between your fingertips to create thin lines from the center to the outer rim of the pastry snake, like the spokes of a wheel. Serve while still warm or at room temperature.

Poached quinces with rose water syrup

Compote de coings

Serves 4

scant 1 cup granulated sugar

1¹/4 cups water

juice of ¹/2 lemon

2 good-size quinces, peeled, seeded, and cut into quarters or thick segments (keep in water with a splash of lemon juice until ready to use, as they discolor very quickly)

2 to 3 tbsp rose water

Poached fruit in syrup is a feature of all Arab-influenced cuisines. Figs, plums, apples, pears, apricots, and oranges are all presented in fragrant syrups to be served with yogurt, cream, or sweet couscous, but quinces are particularly delightful.

Put the sugar and water in a heavy-bottom saucepan and bring to a boil, stirring continuously until the sugar has dissolved. Stir in the lemon juice, reduce the heat, and simmer for 5 to 10 minutes, until the liquid begins to thicken and form a light syrup.

Add the quince pieces, cover, and poach gently for 25 to 30 minutes, until the fruit is tender and has turned pink—the poaching time will vary according to the thickness of the quince pieces.

Stir in the rose water, turn off the heat, and let the quince cool in the saucepan.

Serve chilled or at room temperature.

Gazelles' horns

Kaab el ghzal

Makes 25–30 pastries

Pastry dough

heaping 1³/4 cups all-purpose flour, plus extra for dusting

pinch of salt

2 tbsp butter, melted

1 egg yolk

2 to 3 tbsp orange flower water

¹/4 cup water

sunflower oil, for oiling

Filling

3¹/3 cups ground almonds

scant 1¹/4 cups confectioners' sugar, plus extra for dusting

1 tbsp orange flower water, plus extra for brushing

1 egg white, lightly beaten

3 tbsp butter, melted

1 to 2 tsp ground cinnamon

These sickle-moon-shaped pastries are called "gazelles' horns," as they are said to resemble the horns of the antelope that roam the Atlas mountains. Generally, they are served as a snack with a glass of mint tea or a cold drink, such as almond milk.

Sift the flour with the salt into a bowl. Make a well in the center and pour in the melted butter, egg yolk, orange flower water, and water. Using your fingertips or a palette knife, draw in the flour to form a dough (add more water if the mixture is too dry) and then knead it with your hands. Turn the dough out onto a lightly floured counter and knead until smooth and elastic. Wrap in plastic wrap and chill in the refrigerator for 30 minutes.

Meanwhile, make the filling. Combine all the ingredients in a large bowl and, using your hands, work them into a stiff paste. Take small portions of the mixture and roll into logs about 3 inches/7.5 cm long—you may find it easier to oil your hands so that the paste doesn't stick. Put the logs on a lightly oiled surface. Preheat the oven to 350°F/180°C.

Roll out the dough on a lightly floured counter to form a large rectangle about ¹/16 inch/2 mm thick. Put several almond logs along one long side, 2 inches/5 cm from the edge and leaving a 2-inch/5-cm gap between them. Brush the edges of the dough and around the almond logs with a little water. Fold the edge over the almond logs and press the dough around the filling to keep it in place. Using a fluted pastry wheel, carefully cut a half-moon, starting from the folded edge, around the filling, and back down to the folded edge again, so that you create 3 half-circles. Repeat with the remaining dough until you have about 25 half-circle-shaped pastries.

Put your finger in the center of the bottom edge of each dough and carefully press the filling upward to shape the dough into a crescent moon or a gazelle's horn.

Put the gazelles' horns on a lightly oiled baking sheet and bake in the preheated oven for 15 to 20 minutes, until lightly browned. Transfer to a wire rack. While still hot, brush with a little orange flower water and dust with confectioners' sugar. Serve warm or at room temperature.

Deep-fried orange and honey puffs in syrup

Lokma

Serves 4 to 6

Dough

3 eggs

juice of 1 orange

grated rind of 2 oranges

1/4 cup sunflower oil,
plus extra for deep-frying

2 tbsp runny honey

scant 2 1/4 cups all-purpose flour,
plus extra for handling the dough
and dusting

1 tsp baking powder

Syrup

heaping 1 cup granulated sugar

heaping 1 cup water

juice of 1 lemon

1 to 2 tbsp orange flower water

There are variations on this dish of deep-fried dough bathed in syrup throughout the Islamic world. The Moroccan trademark of fruity flavors makes these puffs unique, as the juice and rind of the oranges enrich the puffs in taste and color.

In a bowl, whisk the eggs with the orange juice and rind and oil until light and frothy, then stir in the honey. Sift the flour with the baking powder and beat it into the egg mixture with a wooden spoon to form a sticky dough. Cover with plastic wrap and let stand at room temperature for 1 hour.

Meanwhile, prepare the syrup. Put the sugar and water in a heavy-bottom saucepan and bring to a boil, stirring continuously, until the sugar has dissolved. Stir in the lemon juice, reduce the heat, and simmer for 10 to 15 minutes, or until the mixture thickens a little and becomes syrupy. Stir in the orange flower water. Keep the syrup warm or reheat when you are cooking the honey puffs.

Beat a heaping tablespoon of flour into the sticky dough until you can handle it with ease and knead it. Turn the dough out onto a lightly floured counter and roll out until about 1/4 inch/5 mm thick. The dough will be very elastic, so keep pulling at it until it stops springing back. Using a pastry cutter, or an inverted glass or jar, cut out equal-sized rounds, 1 to 2 inches/ 2.5 to 5 cm in diameter.

Heat enough oil for deep-frying in a deep-sided saucepan or deep-fat fryer to 350 to 375°F/ 180 to 190°C, or until a cube of bread browns in 30 seconds. Deep-fry the dough rounds, in batches, for 2 minutes, or until golden brown and puffed up. Remove with a slotted spoon and drain on paper towels.

Using tongs, dip each puff in the warm syrup to coat and transfer to a serving platter. Serve immediately.

Sweet couscous with cinnamon and pistachios

Kesksou seffa

Serves 4 to 6

1¼ cups fine couscous

2 tsp ground cinnamon

½ tsp ground cloves

1 to 2 tbsp granulated sugar

1¼ cups boiling water

1 tbsp sunflower oil or melted butter

4 tbsp butter

¾ cup unsalted pistachios

2 to 3 tbsp golden raisins or raisins

½ cup milk

½ cup heavy cream

4 tbsp runny honey

Sweet couscous is popular as a snack, dessert, or nourishing breakfast. Generally, it is served warm or at room temperature. You can add a variety of dried fruits and nuts to the mixture, such as apricots, almonds, and pine nuts.

Put the couscous into a heatproof bowl and stir in the cinnamon, cloves, and sugar. Pour in the boiling water, cover, and set the couscous aside for 10 to 15 minutes to absorb the water.

Drizzle the oil over the couscous. Using your fingertips, rub the oil into the grains to break up the lumps and aerate them.

Melt the butter in a heavy-bottom skillet, add the pistachios, and cook over medium heat, stirring, for 1 to 2 minutes, or until they emit a nutty aroma. Add the golden raisins to the nuts and cook until they have plumped up. Tip over the couscous and toss well. Spoon the couscous into individual bowls.

In a small saucepan, heat the milk and cream together, pour over the couscous in each bowl, and drizzle the honey over the top. Serve immediately, while still warm.

Classic orange salad with orange flower water and dates

Slada bil bortokal

Serves 4 to 6

5 to 6 good-size ripe oranges

1 to 2 tbsp orange flower water

8 moist dried dates, pitted and cut into thin slithers

1 tsp ground cinnamon

This classic dessert is deliciously refreshing and tangy after a rich, spicy meal—the dates add a welcome hint of sweetness at the end. Any sweet oranges will do, and you can use softened, dried apricots, a mango, or golden raisins, instead of dates.

Peel the oranges, making sure you remove all the white pith. Put the peeled oranges on a plate to catch the juice and slice thinly, removing any seeds. Arrange the orange slices in a serving dish.

Tip the juice into a bowl and stir in the orange flower water. Pour the juice mixture over the oranges, cover, and chill in the refrigerator for at least 1 hour.

Just before serving, scatter the date slithers over and around the oranges, and sprinkle the cinnamon over the top—this can be done in lines to form a pattern, if you like.

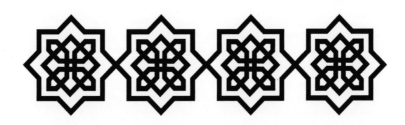

Watermelon and pomegranate salad with rose water and mint

Slada bil dellah

Serves 4 to 6

1 small ripe watermelon or 1 large wedge, about 3 lb 5 oz/1.5 kg

1 ripe pomegranate

2 tbsp rose water

1 to 2 tsp granulated sugar or honey (optional)

fresh mint leaves, for decorating

In many Moroccan households, fresh fruit is often presented as a salad or displayed decoratively on a platter. Honey is occasionally drizzled over tart fruit and the classic scents of rose water or orange flower water are added for a splash of flavor.

Remove the skin and seeds from the watermelon. Put the flesh on a plate to catch the juice and cut it into bite-size cubes. Tip the cubes into a bowl or serving dish.

Cut the pomegranate open on the same plate to catch the juice and scoop out the seeds, discarding any of the bitter membrane and pith. Add the seeds to the watermelon.

Pour the watermelon and pomegranate juices into a bowl and stir in the rose water. Stir in the sugar or honey, if using, until it has dissolved. Pour the scented juice over the fruit and toss lightly. Cover and chill in the refrigerator for at least 1 hour. Scatter the mint leaves over the top to decorate and serve chilled.

Pistachio ice cream with broiled mango slices

Glace de pistache

Serves 4 to 6

1 ripe mango, seeded, peeled, and sliced

confectioners' sugar, for sprinkling

Ice cream

scant 1¼ cups blanched pistachios, finely ground

1¼ cups whole milk

1¼ cups heavy cream

4 egg yolks

scant 1 cup granulated sugar

2 to 3 tbsp rose water or orange flower water

Since the Arab Empire wielded its influence across the Middle East and North Africa, the two ice creams that feature most prominently in these regions are those made with pistachios and almonds.

To make the ice cream, put the ground pistachios, reserving about 2 teaspoons for decorating, in a heavy-bottom saucepan with the milk and cream and bring to a boil.

In a large bowl, beat the egg yolks with the sugar, then pour in the hot milk and cream, beating continuously. Pour the custard mixture back into the saucepan and cook over low heat, stirring continuously, until it thickens, then turn off the heat. Stir in the rose water and let the mixture cool. Pour into a freezerproof container and freeze for 1 hour, or until partially frozen. Remove from the freezer, transfer to a bowl,

and beat to break down the crystals. Freeze the mixture again for 30 minutes, then beat again. Freeze once more, until firm. Alternatively, churn in an ice-cream maker, following the manufacturer's directions.

Remove the ice cream from the freezer and let stand for 10 to 15 minutes before serving. Meanwhile, preheat the broiler to high. Sprinkle the mango slices with confectioners' sugar and broil for 3 to 4 minutes, or until they are slightly caramelized. Serve immediately with scoops of the ice cream, decorated with a sprinkling of the reserved ground pistachios.

Almond milk

Hlib b'louz

Serves 4

scant 1³/4 cups blanched almonds
2¹/2 cups water
¹/2 cup sugar
1 tbsp orange flower water

Enjoyed throughout the Middle East and North Africa, almond milk is nourishing and refreshing. In Morocco, orange flower water or orange rind is added to the drink to give it a floral or zesty lift. This is a delicious drink on a hot day.

Pound the almonds in a mortar with a pestle, or in a blender or food processor, to form a smooth paste—add a splash of water if the paste becomes too stiff.

Put the water and sugar in a heavy-bottom saucepan and bring to a boil, stirring continuously until the sugar has dissolved. Stir in the almond paste, reduce the heat, and simmer for 5 minutes.

Turn off the heat and stir in the orange flower water. Let the mixture cool in the saucepan to enable the flavors to mingle. Strain the mixture through a cheesecloth or a fine, plastic strainer—don't use a metal one, as it will taint the flavor and color of the almonds.

Pour the cloudy liquid into glasses and chill thoroughly in the freezer so that it is almost iced before serving.

Mint tea

Atay bi na'na

Serves 4 to 6

2 tsp Chinese gunpowder green tea
1 small bunch of fresh mint leaves
sugar, to taste

This refreshing tea is Morocco's national drink, offered just about anywhere you go. It is also served at the end of a meal as a digestive. It is prepared by brewing Chinese gunpowder green tea with fresh mint sprigs.

Warm a teapot by adding a little hot water, swirling it around and then discarding the water. Put the tea in the teapot and add the mint leaves and 1 to 2 teaspoons of sugar per person. Pour in boiling water and stir once, then leave to infuse for 5 minutes.

Pour into tea glasses or cups and serve .

Index